MEN
Shining With Youthful
BRILLIANCE

VOLUME 2

MEN
Shining With Youthful
BRILLIANCE

Guidance to the Men
of the SGI-USA

VOLUME 2

DAISAKU IKEDA

World Tribune
—Press—

Santa Monica, California

Published by
World Tribune Press
606 Wilshire Blvd.
Santa Monica, CA 90401

© 2010 by the Soka Gakkai

ISBN 978-1-935523-01-7

Design by Lightbourne, Inc.

Cover photo by Hidenori Fukuma / Sebun Photo of a waterfall in Oirase
Gorge, Aomari Prefecture, Japan.

10 9 8 7 6 5 4 3 2 1

Contents

Editor's Note

This second volume of *Men Shining With Youthful Brilliance* continues to bring together SGI President Daisaku Ikeda's guidance addressed specifically to the men's division of our organization.

As he wrote in his foreword to volume 1: "Kosen-rufu does not exist somewhere in the distance. It is found in your steady, day-to-day accumulation of victories over your own challenging issues in your family, in your career and in your community . . .

"I hope that my men's division members will open up a new golden era of the SGI-USA with profound conviction and the brave heart of a lion king . . . I hope that you will strive patiently, steadfastly and resolutely to build an unshakable 'golden castle of capable people' while cherishing the youth as if they were your own sons and daughters or your own brothers and sisters" (pp. iii–iv).

The citations in this book have been abbreviated as follows:

- WND-1 or 2—refers to *The Writings of Nichiren Daishonin*, volume 1 (Tokyo: Soka Gakkai, 1999) or volume 2 (Tokyo: Soka Gakkai, 2006)

- *Gosho zenshu*—refers to *Nichiren Daishonin gosho zenshu* [The Complete Writings of Nichiren Daishonin], the Japanese-language compilation of Nichiren's writings (Tokyo: Soka Gakkai, 1952)

- OTT—refers to *The Record of the Orally Transmitted Teachings*, translated by Burton Watson (Soka Gakkai: Tokyo, 2004)

SGI–USA Men's Division Mottoes
as
Proud Disciples of SGI President Ikeda

America's Roaring Lions,
Turn Winter into Spring

๛

Disciples, Advance Triumphantly
with Stalwart Resolve

๛

Lion Kings of America,
Seize Resounding Victory

๛

January 2, 2009
Daisaku

THE WATERFALL

The Song of the SGI–USA Men's Division

From the May 24, 2007, speech
Using Our Voices To Accomplish the Buddha's Work

In June 1971, I visited the Oirase Gorge in Aomori Prefecture with a group of representatives from throughout Tohoku Region. Aomori's Tohoku Training Center is now located near the gorge.

Poets find poetry wherever they go. They see something, feel something, and poetry wells up from the depths of their being. This can happen in the middle of the night. Many times, I've had this experience, and my wife has written down the poetry that comes to me spontaneously.

In Tohoku on that day in 1971, I saw a powerfully flowing waterfall. And I composed a poem:

Like the waterfall, fierce
like the waterfall, unflagging
like the waterfall, unfearing
like the waterfall, merrily
like the waterfall, proudly—
a man should have the bearing of a king.

Many years later, in June 1994, I was presented with an honorary doctorate from Scotland's famous University of Glasgow. A solemn and magnificent conferral ceremony was conducted in the historic hall of this pioneering institution of higher learning. The entire event was truly impressive. It was an unparalleled honor. Those accompanying me as well were all deeply moved by the proceedings.

Dr. J. Forbes Munro, the university's clerk of senate, delivered the award citation, in which he quoted my poem about the waterfall at Oirase Gorge. He had come across the poem in a volume of my verses that have been translated into English by the respected translator Burton Watson. Dr. Munro decided that this poem was a fitting description of my own life. When he finished his wonderful speech, loud applause rang throughout the hall.

On the weekend of May 19–20, 2007, Dr. Munro, who was in Japan for an extended visit, traveled to Aomori Prefecture, where I composed the poem . . . Men's division members of Aomori's Constant Victory Sub-Prefecture, which encompasses Towada and Misawa cities, welcomed Dr. Munro by singing a choral version of "The Waterfall." I understand that Dr. Munro was touched by this gesture.

(June 29, 2007, World Tribune, *p. 2)*

FROM THE JUNE 16, 2009, SPEECH
OPEN THE WAY TO VICTORY

WITH THE ROYAL BEARING OF CHAMPIONS described in this poem ("The Waterfall"), may you be the kind of people whom others praise as having made a difference—for instance, whose presence helped them move their lives in a positive direction or was vital in the success of an activity or was pivotal in building a more solid organization.

(July 17, 2009, World Tribune, *p. 5)*

The Waterfall

poem by Daisaku Ikeda

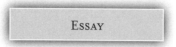

The Courageous Champions of the Men's Division

FROM THE ESSAY SERIES
OUR BRILLIANT PATH TO VICTORY
BY SHIN'ICHI YAMAMOTO[1]

Courageous champions—
overcome the storms of hardship
and create history.

The English poet Alfred Tennyson writes:

Come, my friends,
'Tis not too late to seek a newer world.
Push off, and sitting well in order smite
The sounding furrows.[2]

THE WAVES BUFFETING SOCIETY rage high and the winds of economic turmoil blow fierce. Our men's division members, the noble captains of kosen-rufu, are each striving valiantly in their own personal spheres of responsibility, leading the way forward through these perilous waters.

Nichiren Daishonin writes: "Only the ship of Myoho-renge-kyo enables one to cross the sea of the sufferings of birth and death" (WND-1, 33). We uphold the Mystic Law, which enables us to surmount life's challenges and chart a course for a life of tremendous joy.

At the recent Nationwide Men's Division Leaders Meeting, held in conjunction with the Soka Gakkai Headquarters Leaders Meeting (on March 6, 2010), I asked for a representative from Africa to come up on stage and lead the final cheer. A men's division chapter leader from Côte d'Ivoire responded to my call. Originally the captain of a merchant shipping vessel, this chapter leader is affectionately called "Captain" by his friends. Unfortunately, the shipping company for which he worked closed down. He looked for a new job but was unable to find one right away. After eight months of job hunting and intense chanting, he finally found a position at an oil company. Today, he is the head of the company's sales office, brilliantly demonstrating proof of changing poison into medicine.

There are currently more than 20,000 members of SGI-Côte d'Ivoire, and the membership keeps growing. They are all devoting themselves earnestly for kosen-rufu, upholding as their mottoes: "Always ready to fight alongside Sensei!" "Always ready to make true friends!" "Always ready to fight injustice!"

At that meeting, I exchanged a firm handshake with the brave chapter leader from Africa and asked him to pass on my best regards to all his fellow members back home.

When my mentor Josei Toda's businesses hit hard times, I worked with utter dedication to support him. I strove with all my might to overcome the crisis and pave the way for Mr. Toda to be inaugurated as the second Soka Gakkai president. And then, with selfless dedication to propagating the Law, I threw myself into achieving Mr. Toda's cherished goal of 750,000 member households. In every struggle that I have waged to help establish the correct teaching for the peace of the land, I have won victory after victory. Though in poor health myself, I assisted Mr. Toda, giving my all day after day, fully prepared to lay down my life without the slightest regret in order to make his vision a reality.

One day in March 1955, in the midst of our unrelenting struggles, Mr. Toda said to me: "Didn't we fight courageously, you and I!"

I felt I could receive no higher honor than these words.

In the same spirit, I'd now like to say to our men's division members: "Together, let's fight courageously!"

In the early morning hours of March 16, 1958, some six thousand youth eagerly gathered at the foot of Mount Fuji to attend a commemorative gathering for kosen-rufu that would come to represent a timeless ceremony of passing the baton from mentor to disciple. Though March marked the start of spring, the mornings were still very cold, and everyone's breaths came out in white puffs. The young people all cheered when, unexpectedly, they were served steaming hot pork soup. Mr. Toda, concerned about their early morning arrival, had personally arranged for the soup to be made, thinking that the youth would need something to warm them up.

Two men's division members, mainstays of Kamata Chapter, were in charge of the preparations. They were proud to be doing this for the youth. Standing by the four large simmering vats, they worked furiously to divide the soup into smaller wooden tubs for distribution. Soup was then ladled into the bowls everyone had brought along with them. The youth blew on the hot broth to cool it as they ate appreciatively. While the soup itself warmed their bodies, their mentor's concern for them warmed their hearts even more. Their mentor's pork soup became one of their golden memories.

Like a father who, out of concern for his children, quietly supports them, Mr. Toda was always thinking about what he could do for the youth. When it's cold, hot food can warm the body and help prevent one from catching a chill.

I strive to emulate Mr. Toda's behavior, chanting wholeheartedly each day for the health and victory of all our members, particularly the youth of such behind-the-scenes groups as the Soka Group, Gajokai and Byakuren who are doing their utmost to support members in northern regions at this cold time of year. I'd also like to express my gratitude to the sincere men's division members who are also working in various behind-the-scenes groups, as well as the deliverers of the *Seikyo Shimbun,* the Soka Gakkai's daily newspaper in Japan.

I hope our men's division members not only take courageous action on the front lines of our movement but also forge themselves into compassionate leaders who truly understand the hearts of their fellow members. That is the key for them to develop the noble character of genuine champions of faith.

Become
an invincible pillar
and achieve
a life of
indestructible victory.

The men's division was established on March 5, 1966. The skies were clear as 750 representatives gathered at the Soka Gakkai Headquarters in Tokyo for a ceremony to establish the division. I was also present for this joyous new beginning.

Nichiren famously states: "In battles soldiers regard the general as their soul. If the general were to lose heart, his soldiers would become cowards" (WND-1, 613). When men in the prime of life brim with energy and vigor, they can be a vital driving force for growth and victory in their families, workplaces and communities. Also, in the organization, when the men's division is solid, the women's, young women's and young men's divisions can carry out their activities with confidence and peace of mind.

"Men's division members, golden pillars supporting and protecting the precious Soka family, be strong and self-assured!" This was, without a doubt, the wish of Mr. Makiguchi and Mr. Toda, who both took the lead for kosen-rufu in middle age and beyond. I established the men's division in order to realize the vision of these two mentors.

The day after the inaugural men's division meeting was held, I left on a trip to North and South America to encourage our members there. I stopped in Los Angeles and New York, and on March 10, I flew to Brazil. Looking out of the airplane window, I saw the light of the sun illuminating the horizon as the great Amazon River stretched out below. The formation of the men's division was the final touch needed to set in motion a flow of global kosen-rufu as powerful and majestic as the mighty Amazon.

In later years, I had the fortune to meet with Amadeu Thiago de Mello, the renowned Brazilian environmental activist and poet of the Amazon (in Tokyo in April 1997). On that occasion, he composed this impromptu poem:

I work with love and song
toward building the future.

The important thing is not just surviving,
but contributing to change,
each in our own way,
in our own community.[3]

These words perfectly describe the spirit of the men's division members.

I once presented some words of the Daishonin to the members of the Taiyo-kai (Sun Group) and Kanto-kai (Fighting Spirit Group) [groups in Japan comprised of men's division members who have retired from their jobs and now participate in kosen-rufu activities during the day]: "A lantern [can light] up a place that has been dark for a hundred, a thousand, or ten thousand years" (WND-1, 923). Many of the men's division members have overcome great challenges in their lives. They are courageous and have practical knowledge.

They serve as beacons that light the way forward for others and guide their juniors in a positive direction.

We live in a time when people are becoming more and more alienated from one another. Men who can offer warm and open-hearted encouragement, rather than those who are merely dignified and silent, truly shine with a golden light. All of our men's division members have faces that are etched with character. But there is a difference between weathering hardships and being arrogant. The important thing is to care for others, reach out to them and talk with them, not becoming surly or conceited. Such sincere behavior is the first sure step toward creating a happy family and advancing kosen-rufu in the local community. For men, the key to positive change lies in their immediate environment.

The Russian author Leo Tolstoy writes: "The meaning of life can only be found in bringing people together. When we embrace this belief, we cannot help but work wholeheartedly to fulfill our individual responsibilities, and we cannot help but treat everyone we encounter with consideration, kindness, and love."[4] It doesn't matter if you're not famous or renowned in society. Nothing is nobler in life than being appreciated and valued by many people around you for your sincerity and support.

Japanese society is aging. No one can escape the four universal sufferings of human existence—birth, aging, sickness and death. Nichiren Buddhism is the great teaching that enables us to transform these fundamental sufferings into the four noble virtues of eternity, happiness, true self and purity.

Nichiren writes to his disciple Shijo Kingo, who is a forerunner of today's men's division members: "The wonderful means of truly putting an end to the physical and spiritual obstacles of all living beings is none other than Nam-myoho-renge-kyo" (WND-1, 842).

The time has come when men's division members, great seekers and practitioners of the Mystic Law, are being looked on as a solid source of reliance and support in their communities.

Now is the time to stand up!
Now is the time to take initiative and act with courage and self-confidence!

How wonderful it is
to have
a clear purpose—
this is the mark
of a hope-filled champion.

Rise into action
as leaders in faith,
emulating lofty Mount Fuji.

My mentor, second Soka Gakkai president Josei Toda, was an unparalleled leader of kosen-rufu. As his dedicated disciple, I worked alongside him more closely than anyone. In the process, I learned the practical requirements that are especially important for men to develop into great leaders.

As an expression of my high hopes for the newly established men's division (in March 1966), I titled an editorial for the Soka Gakkai study journal *Daibyakurenge,* "Outstanding Leaders of the Mystic Law."[5] What is the key requirement for our "outstanding leaders" of the men's division to spearhead the way to victory in this year of the Soka Gakkai's eightieth anniversary? It is the indomitable strength to fight and take action in order to achieve even the most challenging goals. And what is the source of that strength? It is found in employing the unrivaled strategy of the Lotus Sutra, in chanting Nam-myoho-renge-kyo, which is like the roar of a lion (see WND-1, 119).

It is also particularly important to be specific in what we chant about. Nichiren Daishonin even tells us: "Though one might point at the earth and miss it, . . . it could never come about that the prayers of the practitioner of the Lotus Sutra would go unanswered" (WND-1, 345). That's all the more reason we need to chant with clearly defined goals, rather than chanting aimlessly without direction, and make a firm vow to achieve them without fail. That way we'll definitely experience surefire actual proof of faith, just as first Soka Gakkai president Tsunesaburo Makiguchi assured us.

Let's chant for every single one of our fellow members to enjoy happiness, good health, financial fortune and personal security. Let's chant for kosen-rufu in our communities to advance and expand. Let's chant for the way to victory to unfold limitlessly for our movement. Let's keep chanting Nam-myoho-renge-kyo strongly and resonately with specific goals in mind, morning and evening, until we achieve them. And let's continue chanting each day, praying wholeheartedly for the happiness of individual fellow members and the growth of the youth, and eagerly participate in activities at the forefront of our movement.

It's vital that we follow our prayers with action, heeding Nichiren's call that we exert ourselves unceasingly in our Buddhist practice and also speak out intrepidly for what is right.

I hope that you, the men's division members, whether at your workplaces or within your local Gakkai organizations, will become trusted individuals who have the capacity to take responsibility for everyone's happiness and success with the heart of a lion king.

Our true strength is manifested when we, as individuals, summon forth the courage to take responsibility for whatever challenges arise, without running away.

The German poet and playwright Friedrich von Schiller declared that the strongest of all are those who are strong when they stand alone.[6] These words have always inspired me. They describe the spirit of the men's division.

Let's reach out to those in our environment and steadily expand our warm, humanistic network one by one.

Live your life fully
with strength, joy and no regrets,
resolutely walking
the great path
of truth and justice.

At this time of unprecedented economic turmoil, the men's division members have stepped up their efforts to conduct home visits and offer support and encouragement to their fellow members. Countless dramas of men bravely taking on the challenge of changing their karma through practicing Nichiren Buddhism are unfolding across the country.

In January 2010, the men's division and young men's division members in Hokkaido (the northernmost of Japan's four main islands), undaunted by the winter cold, united to hold a series of Buddhist introductory meetings centered on sharing experiences in faith. These were held at a total of 730 locations throughout Hokkaido—a place that, incidentally, has profound ties to the first three presidents and this year celebrates the fifty-fifth anniversary of the Otaru Debate.[7]

Among the speakers at one of these meetings was a seventy-five-year-old group leader who related his experience of recently starting a new part-time job. Another was a member who was laid off when his company went through restructuring but was able to turn this setback around, finding a new job at a new company and eventually becoming its president. There was also a district leader who valiantly strove to introduce Nichiren's teachings to others while he himself battled a serious illness. He declared that his illness had given him new appreciation for the greatness of Nichiren Buddhism.

Men's division and young men's division members in Miyagi Prefecture in the Tohoku region,[8] a bastion of many outstanding leaders of kosen-rufu, have also been holding similar meetings.

In this way, the men of Soka have been showing great creativity in organizing seminars and meetings that inspire and encourage members and guests alike.

In addition, the men's division members have won wide appreciation throughout the organization for taking the lead in efforts to promote *Seikyo Shimbun* readership nationwide.

Through their work and community connections, many men's division members possess a vast circle of friends and acquaintances.

The energetic activities of the men's division are an immense source of inspiration, courage and assurance for members throughout our organization.

The men's division has stood up! Courageous lions have risen into action!

In *The Record of the Orally Transmitted Teachings,* we find this profound passage: "Forbearance is the Land of Eternally Tranquil Light. This mind of forbearance is called Shakyamuni Buddha" (OTT, 169). In other words, the essential strength of the Buddha lies in possessing a spirit of forbearance to endure every form of hardship and adversity. If we are fainthearted and never experience hardships, we cannot bring forth the power of the Buddha. Another name for the Buddha is "Hero of the World." How can we be heroes of this world without understanding its trials and sufferings? To have forbearance means to be fearless, undaunted and unshaken by the difficulties we may encounter in this troubled, strife-filled world in which we live. The spirit of forbearance pulses with the power, wisdom and life-force of the Buddha.

The world of Buddhahood exists in the nine worlds. It is, therefore, by challenging the sufferings and hardships of the nine worlds through faith in the Mystic Law that the world of Buddhahood wells forth from within us.

Ultimately, Buddhism is about winning. It is important, therefore, that you win in your struggles. A steady stream of capable youth is sure to be inspired by your admirable example and follow your lead. Please demonstrate to your children and the youth the great actual proof of faith gained by those who serve as golden pillars of kosen-rufu. The youth are looking up to you with pride and are counting on your continued valiant efforts.

Men have great strength. They have a rich fund of wisdom to win out over difficult times. They have the trust that they've earned as responsible members of society.

Men's division members: With courageous faith, please open this great storehouse of treasures you possess!

When a sense of helplessness pervades society and everyone else has given up on finding solutions to seemingly impossible challenges, it is time for men of character and substance to stand up.

In the early second half of the eighteenth century, America was still a British colony. Though the people of America were dissatisfied with their situation, the "common sense" that prevailed was that they had no choice but to follow the orders of their colonial rulers. Thomas Paine, writer and political activist of the American Revolution, broke through that atmosphere of deadlock and made a case for a new, genuine common sense based on independence and freedom. With his 1776 pamphlet, *Common Sense,* the flame of the struggle was lit.

Paine writes: "Of more worth is one honest man to society . . . than all the crowned ruffians that ever lived."[9] He also said: "O ye that love mankind! Ye that dare oppose, not only the tyranny, but the tyrant, stand forth!"[10] These words ignited the hearts of the people and rallied their determination to win their independence. The road to that goal was thus widely opened.

Paine was thirty-nine when he wrote *Common Sense,* the age of many of our younger men's division members. He continued to fight for justice and liberty throughout his life and even endured imprisonment. What was his strength? It was the fact that he was an ordinary person.

Paine was born into a craftsman's family. Later in life, he experienced failure in business and also lost his first wife less than a year after they were married. He lived in relative poverty, but that made him especially aware of the thoughts and feelings of the people. He volunteered as a member of America's Continental Army and joined the struggle for independence.

True champions not only rally others but put themselves in the heart of the struggle and fight harder than anyone.

Paine writes: "It is not in numbers, but in unity, that our great strength lies."[11] When he made his solitary stand, both young and old alike followed. Together they broke through what once prevailed as "common sense" and made the impossible possible.

The courage and actions of men can create a solidarity that leads to a resounding victory.

Yamaoka Tesshu was a pioneering leader of Japan's Meiji Restoration (1868). He met and directly negotiated with statesman and military leader Saigo Takamori, helping open the way for the bloodless surrender of Edo Castle, stronghold of the Tokugawa shogunate.

Yamaoka experienced great hardships in his life: the loss of both parents in his teens, the upheavals that roiled Japanese society in his youth, and painful episodes of self-doubt. In his later years, he wrote the following poem while looking up at the snowcapped peak of Mount Fuji:

Whether sunny
or cloudy,
the essential form
of Mount Fuji—one and unique—
never changes.[12]

Yamaoka was unconcerned by the caprices of public opinion. He had made up his mind to proceed boldly on the path of his mission, remaining as unshakable as Mount Fuji. His heart was resolute; nothing could sway or deter him from his course. Right up until his death, he dedicated himself to fostering leaders of the younger generation while continuing to study and work on his own self-development. Saigo Takamori described him as a man who was "selfless, unattached to fame, rank, or wealth."[13]

People who are unhindered by ambition for fame or profit, who have utterly dedicated their lives to their chosen mission based on their firm belief that "the treasures of the heart are the most valuable of all" (WND-1, 851), shine with an enduring golden light.

The passion of youth is wonderful, but passion for a cause that remains undimmed through one's forties, fifties, sixties, seventies and eighties is the genuine article. As long as there are individuals who are determined to take the lead in achieving victory for kosen-rufu with the resolve that they themselves are the Soka Gakkai, the future of our organization will be secure.

I still remember a stormy day shortly after I was inaugurated as the third Soka Gakkai president. A member from Saitama Prefecture rushed to my rickety house in Kobayashi-cho in Tokyo's Ota Ward. "Sensei, is everything okay? I'm here. I'll keep you safe!" he cried. It turned out that he had traveled all the way by bicycle in the rain to see if I was all right. Today, he remains an active member of the men's division, his eyes still shining brightly as he continues to work with vigor on the front lines of kosen-rufu now as then.

Champions rich in wisdom,
together pave and walk
the brilliant path leading
to long, healthy,
and fulfilling lives.

I once presented this poem to the men's division members in Osaka. We have the path our mentor has opened for us. We have friends to walk it with us. The ultimate fulfillment is found in following this sublime path.

A strong backbone of integrity, arising from deep commitment to repaying one's debts of gratitude, runs through the lives of those who advance together with their mentor and genuine comrades in faith.

Kosen-rufu is a noble endeavor to realize peace and happiness for all humankind. It is the highest and noblest purpose to which we can dedicate our lives wholeheartedly and without regret.

Let's advance along the lofty path of the shared commitment of mentor and disciple! Let's climb the magnificent and yet unexplored mountains of kosen-rufu!

Of the six senior priests, Nichiren's loyal disciple Nikko Shonin alone taught, shared and spread the Daishonin's teaching faithfully without the slightest error or deviation. When he was eighty-eight, he composed for posterity "The Twenty-six Admonitions of Nikko."[14]

Abutsu-bo, a follower who had a profound seeking spirit in faith, traveled all the way from Sado in spite of his advanced age to visit the Daishonin at Mount Minobu. The older he became, the harder Abutsu-bo fought with the youthful determination that Buddhism means being victorious.

The spirit of Nikko Shonin and Abutsu-bo is perfectly mirrored in the members of our Many Treasures Group (which is equivalent to the SGI-USA Golden Stage Group for members age sixty and above).

The Chinese poet Du Fu writes: "A man's efforts come to fruition in old age."[15] The true measure of our life is revealed in its final years by the finishing touches we put on it and what we have actually accomplished.

In a work written when he was fifty-seven, Nichiren declares: "Only this great teaching [Nam-myoho-renge-kyo] will spread throughout the entire land of Jambudvipa [the whole world]" (WND-1, 896). When Mr. Makiguchi was fifty-seven, he began practicing Nichiren Buddhism. He wrote down his feelings at the time, saying: "With an indescribable joy, I completely changed the way I had lived for almost sixty years."

Mr. Toda was nineteen when he encountered Mr. Makiguchi, and he was forty-five when he learned that his mentor had died in prison. Having awoken to his mission as a Bodhisattva of the Earth, he became an indomitable champion of the Mystic Law and vowed to show the world the greatness and integrity of his mentor. This was the beginning of his full-fledged struggle for kosen-rufu.

I, too, encountered my mentor at the age of nineteen and triumphed in an unending series of challenging struggles on the path of kosen-rufu. Now, at eighty-two (in 2010), I am healthier than I've ever been. This is in large part due, I'm sure, to the earnest prayers of our women's division members. I'm filled with a life-force as vital as any youth. This is because I have a great mentor in Mr. Toda. It is also because I continue to challenge myself with an ever youthful spirit as his dedicated disciple based on the principle of true cause, always moving forward from the present moment on. And it is because I am devoting myself to spreading the Mystic Law, which is the source of perennial youth and an eternally vibrant life-force, together with countless young successors who will carry on our proud movement in the future.

In a famous passage from "The Heritage of the Ultimate Law of Life," Nichiren states: "Gold can be neither burned by fire nor corroded or swept away by water . . . You are like pure gold" (WND-1, 217). My fellow members of the men's division, comrades in the struggle for kosen-rufu—particularly those of my generation who have been striving together with me the longest in this lifetime! You, my precious friends, people of pure gold who share profound ties and are forging a magnificent legacy of joint struggle! Just as gold is never corroded, be indestructible golden pillars, cherishing and protecting the people and helping them shine, come what may! Dedicate the rest of your noble lives to realizing the great vow of kosen-rufu, together with me and your fellow members! Therein lies a life of unparalleled joy, honor and fulfillment.

> *Today again, take action,*
> *confident that it will infuse*
> *your life with eternal benefit.*
> *Cheerfully endure all hardships*
> *and win without fail!*

(July 9, 2010, World Tribune*)*

1 *Shin'ichi Yamamoto is a pen name of SGI President Daisaku Ikeda.*
2 *Alfred Tennyson, "Ulysses," in* The Complete Poetical Works of Alfred Tennyson *(Boston: James R. Osgood and Company, 1876), p. 80.*
3 *From an article in* Seikyo Shimbun, *April 26, 1997.*
4 *Translated from Russian.* Pis'ma *(Letters) in* Lev Tolstoi: Polnoe sobranie sochinenii *(Complete Works of Lev Tolstoy), (Moscow: TERRA, 1992), vol. 63, p. 384.*
5 Daibyakurenge, *April 1966 issue.*
6 *Translated from German. Friedrich von Schiller,* Wilhelm Tell, *in* Sämmtliche Werke *(Complete Works), (Stuttgart: J. G. Cotta'schen Buchhandlung, 1838), vol. 6, p. 28.*
7 *A public debate between Soka Gakkai representatives and priests of Nichiren Shu (the Minobu school of Nichiren Buddhism), held at the Otaru Civic Hall in the city of Otaru, Hokkaido, on March 11, 1955. The debate was won by the Soka Gakkai side. The incident is described in detail in volume nine of* The Human Revolution.
8 *The Tohoku region comprises Aomori, Akita, Iwate, Miyagi, Yamagata and Fukushima prefectures, which are located in the northern part of the Japanese main island of Honshu.*

9 Thomas Paine, *"Common Sense,"* in Thomas Paine: Collected Writings *(New York: The Library of America, 1995), p. 20.*

10 Ibid., p. 36.

11 Ibid.

12 Translated from Japanese. Ryohei Kamiwatari, Shumpu wo Kiru: Shosetsu Yamaoka Tesshu *(Living in Turbulent Times: Yamaoka Tesshu, a Novel), (Tokyo: PHP Kenkyujo, 2000), p. 334.*

13 Ibid., p. 248.

14 *"The Twenty-six Admonitions of Nikko": A document that Nikko Shonin, Nichiren Daishonin's designated successor, wrote for the sake of both priests and laity of future generations to maintain the purity of Nichiren's teachings. It outlines the fundamental spirit of faith, practice and study.*

15 Translated from Japanese. Kojiro Yoshikawa, Toho Shi Chu *(Annotated Poems of Du Fu), (Tokyo: Chikuma Shobo, 1977), vol. 1, p. 59.*

EXCERPT

Confidently Sharing Our Ideals and Convictions With Others

FROM THE MARCH 6, 2010, SPEECH

CONGRATULATIONS ON TODAY'S high-spirited Men's Division Leaders Meeting!

The women's division is delighted and the youth division is astonished to see the men's division so active around the country! *[Laughter.]*

I know you are really challenging yourselves in these difficult economic times. As our golden pillars, I hope you'll draw on your rich fund of experience to support the women's and young women's division members and warmly help foster the young men's division members.

Especially for those of you in the men's division who have received rigorous training in the youth division, now is the time to put that training to full use. Rather than telling the young men what they should do, lead by setting an inspiring example yourself. The present is crucial. I'm counting on you, the men's division members, to stand up in earnest. If you continue working to advance kosen-rufu, contributing in your unique way with undiminished enthusiasm and a youthful spirit, your juniors will naturally follow your lead. I hope you will always warmly encourage the youth. Make a lasting impression on them through your personal example of selfless devotion to kosen-rufu and the welfare of your fellow members.

I have given my all for kosen-rufu with that resolve for more than five decades. I assisted and supported my mentor, Josei Toda, to the fullest extent of my ability. I can pledge before the Gohonzon without hesitation that I don't have a single regret.

Broadening Our Network of Good

In the early days of our movement, there were many longstanding leaders working alongside Mr. Toda, but he entrusted everything to the youth in order to achieve a breakthrough in the deadlock we had reached in our propagation efforts. I was in my twenties then. "Daisaku, will you take the lead?" he asked me. "Yes!" I replied instantly. Filled with an ardent wish to respond to my mentor, I strove tirelessly to share Nichiren Buddhism with many others and also to rebuild Mr. Toda's businesses.

That was the start of the Soka Gakkai's dynamic development, like the sun rising majestically into the sky. From that point, our movement took off with incredible momentum. We have advanced with that energy to this day.

In any age, youth are always the key—youth whose hearts shine with the spirit of mentor and disciple.

Mr. Toda insisted that nothing is worse than cowardice. Each individual, he said, needs to cultivate the dignity of a lion king. And he added that if each of us isn't strong and committed to the welfare of others and society, everyone will suffer.

There is no need whatsoever for the youth to hold back or be shy. I'm counting on you, the youth, to wage a decisive, lionhearted struggle. Men's division members, please support them!

When we exert ourselves in our noble Buddhist practice with the humble spirit to give our all to supporting and encouraging the youth, we will accumulate immense benefit. All of our hard work will become a precious treasure in our lives.

Mr. Makiguchi and Mr. Toda were men's division members, and I, too, am a men's division member. The Daishonin noted that, in battles, courageous generals are crucial to victory (see WND-1,

613). Let's strive with courage and win! Mr. Toda's words still resonate in my heart: "In a struggle against the unjust or corrupt, you must win! Widen your circle of trustworthy, good-hearted friends day by day, and expand it year after year!" I hope that you, my successors, will also engrave these words in your heart.

Arrogance destroys Buddhism. To treat people with contempt, seek personal advantage at the expense of others, collude with corrupt authorities and persecute the good and just is truly reprehensible behavior. It is through waging a committed struggle against such arrogant individuals and triumphing over them that we can reveal our Buddhahood.

The corrupt are quick to band together in their shared ambitions. That is why it is vital that we continue to broaden our network of good in order to counteract such forces and ensure that truth and justice prevail.

"Where There Is Unseen Virtue, There Will Be Visible Reward"

Today, Shunzo Ohno of the SGI-USA arts division is also attending. I'm happy to see you! Thank you for joining us!

Mr. Ohno is a world-famous jazz trumpeter who has won two Grammys. He's presented me with a number of his CDs, and I listen to his music almost every day. When I do, I always offer a prayer for the happiness of our members in the United States and around the world. I'm thrilled to observe Mr. Ohno's successful career as an internationally acclaimed musician. I wish to wholeheartedly applaud and commend him today for his wonderful achievements as an arts division representative.

I treasure above all the sincerity of members who strive alongside me with a shared commitment for kosen-rufu. I have the highest respect and admiration for those who work hard behind the scenes, who exert themselves earnestly. In this respect, too, I would like to offer my deepest gratitude to Mr. Ohno. Thank you!

[Mr. Ohno responded to President Ikeda's words, saying that he would make a fresh start from that day and strive to show further actual proof of faith, doing his utmost to advance kosen-rufu.]

I'm touched by your words.

Mr. Ohno originally hails from Chubu region,[1] one of the Gakkai's strongest bastions. In his youth, he also received training as a member of the Brass Band and valiantly challenged himself in Soka Group responsibilities, showing himself to be a courageous champion of kosen-rufu. Today, he is an SGI-USA chapter leader. Last year, his chapter introduced ten new members to Nichiren Buddhism.

Mr. Ohno has experienced many daunting trials and obstacles. His front teeth were broken in a car accident, a terrible injury for a trumpet player. He also underwent surgery for throat cancer, facing another threat that could have ended his artistic career. But he triumphed over these adversities based on his strong faith. It is now fourteen years since he had surgery, and the cancer has not returned. How wonderful!

His concert tour in Japan last year, celebrating the thirty-fifth anniversary of his move to the United States, was a great success. He continues to enjoy the highest esteem as a world-class artist. He is truly a winner in life who exemplifies the words: "Where there is unseen virtue, there will be visible reward" (WND-1, 907).

[Addressing Mr. Ohno, who turned sixty last year:] Life starts at sixty! I pray for your good health and for your continued success and victory in life!

At the 38th Soka Gakkai Headquarters Leaders Meeting, held in conjunction with the Nationwide Men's Division Leaders Meeting, at the Makiguchi Memorial Hall in Hachioji, Tokyo.

1 *In the Soka Gakkai organization, Chubu region encompasses Aichi, Mie and Gifu prefectures. Mr. Ohno was born in Gifu.*

ESSAY

Men: Champions of Kosen-rufu

DECEMBER 18, 2008

I watch on
as you grow
into a towering tree
undaunted by storms
or blizzards.

I ONCE SENT THIS POEM TO A YOUNG FRIEND who had fallen ill. When I first received word that he was battling illness, I immediately took up my pen and wrote a note of encouragement for him. This particular young man overcame his illness and has grown to be as resilient as a towering tree. He has become an excellent and compassionate leader.

In the beautiful pageant of the four seasons, perhaps the ginkgo tree is second only to the cherry in the vivid impression it makes on us. Its golden leaves shining in the cold winds of early December announce the completion of the year. When I gaze up at the ginkgo trees, I am reminded of the noble and stately presence of our men's division members. The avenue of ginkgo trees in Tokyo's Aoyama neighborhood (near the Soka Gakkai Headquarters in Shinanomachi, Tokyo) is one of the city's popular sights. This year (2008), those ginkgo trees greeted their hundredth year.

Every day, people pass along the road beneath these venerable trees, talking together and looking up at the ginkgos as they go about their daily business. For me, this road is filled with unforgettable memories—indeed, it is a road of unforgettable significance in the history of kosen-rufu.

The 146 trees lining the avenue were planted there by the pioneering park and landscape designer Yoshinobu Orishimo. The trees are trimmed to match the gentle slope of the road, employing the principle of perspective to create a world-famous view.

In 1999, a cutting of one of these ginkgo trees was grafted onto an old tree at Humboldt University in Germany as part of the effort to green up Berlin, the new capital of the reunified nation.

The eminent German author Johann Wolfgang von Goethe once wrote that the ginkgo leaf "uplifts the one who knows." Apparently, Goethe's garden included a ginkgo, a tree that was introduced to Europe from Asia.

At present, construction is proceeding smoothly on the new Soka University Silk Road, an avenue that will be lined with cherry and ginkgo trees at the school. Soon, youthful Goethes of the twenty-first century will talk together as they walk along this path, gazing up from time to time at these splendid trees.

Ginkgos are said to have a powerful life force—one that has enabled the species to survive for more than 200 million years. They flourished from the days of the dinosaurs and weathered the ice ages. As one of the world's oldest species, they've been called "living fossils." They are vigorous trees with a strong resistance to insect damage and disease, as well as many pollutants. What impressive and magnificent trees they are.

I fondly recall someone telling me in my youth that placing a ginkgo leaf between the pages of a book would prevent bookworms from destroying the pages. One day soon after the end of World War II, I took three fallen ginkgo leaves that I had picked up in Aoyama and used them as bookmarks in Walt Whitman's *Leaves of Grass*, a collection of poems I was reading. Those ginkgo leaves, together with that favorite book, were always close at hand.

Japan's ginkgos originate from China. In Japanese, there is another word for ginkgo that is written with Chinese characters that literally mean "grandfather-grandchild tree," because the fruits of a ginkgo tree one plants will be harvested by one's grandchildren. I read this explanation once long ago and never forgot it. To me, that name seems to say: "I'm not living for myself but for the sake of the generations that will come after me. I'll bring forth my life force to the fullest and achieve great things." When I look at a tall ginkgo tree, I think about the people of previous generations who planted and cared for it.

I was born in Tokyo. From the time of my youth, I was proud of the fact that the ginkgo is our official city tree. I was later delighted to learn that the ginkgo is also the official tree of both Osaka and Kanagawa prefectures, places with which I have close ties.

Ginkgo-lined Yamashita Park Avenue in front of our Kanagawa Culture Center, which overlooks the harbor in Yokohama, has been chosen as one of the one hundred most beautiful streets in Japan. A row of tall ginkgo trees also adorns the site of our Tohoku Culture Center in Sendai, Miyagi Prefecture.

As the Japanese poet Takuboku Ishikawa, who hailed from the Tohoku region, wrote, "A towering ginkgo tree raises its golden arms up into the clear skies, like a mighty giant." This verse makes me think of my friends in the men's division who also stand tall, like golden pillars, triumphing over storms and blizzards, in every corner of the world.

I once wrote to a men's division member from Tokyo's Minato Ward, where the ginkgo trees in Aoyama are, "Like the ginkgo tree, standing firm and resolute against the winter winds, live proudly, firmly rooted in bold and resolute faith."

"More valuable than treasures in a storehouse are the treasures of the body, and the treasures of the heart are the most valuable of all" (WND-1, 851). Nichiren Daishonin wrote these words to his disciple Shijo Kingo, who was persecuted because of his faith and struggled valiantly against the hardships that assailed him in the turbulent society of his day.

"Treasures in a storehouse" refer to money and economic power. "Treasures of the body" refer to health and occupational skills, as well as social standing, trust in the community and recognition. For several years, Shijo Kingo had been facing challenges on all of these fronts.

Shijo Kingo fully persevered through the harshest of adversities that, in terms of his career, entailed a battle deciding life or death, victory or defeat. For him, each day was a do-or-die struggle permitting no lapse in judgment or effort.

For his part, Nichiren pointed out to his beloved disciple how to live wisely and, at the same time, heartily encouraged him, as if to say: "You possess the treasures of the heart. What have you to fear? You can triumph through the strongest force of all, the shared faith of mentor and disciple!"

The treasures of the storehouse and the treasures of the body ebb and flow with time, but the treasures of the heart—gained through upholding the eternal Mystic Law—never can be destroyed. That is why SGI members have accumulated the greatest treasures of the heart in all the world.

In these last busy days of the year, I am sure that many of our members are urgently grappling with problems brought on by the once-in-a-century financial crisis we are now facing. I am painfully aware of how difficult this is. The anguish felt by members who are fighting with all their might to survive these hard times strikes to the very depths of my own heart. My empathy comes from the experiences I had working for second Soka Gakkai president Josei Toda when his businesses fell into dire financial straits, a time when I valiantly strove alone to support my mentor and resolve that desperate situation.

Nichiren writes, "I am praying that, no matter how troubled the times may become, the Lotus Sutra and the ten demon daughters will protect all of you, praying as earnestly as though to produce fire from damp wood, or to obtain water from parched ground" (WND-1, 444).

With this passage firmly in mind, my wife and I are earnestly chanting Nam-myoho-renge-kyo for the sake of all our precious members.

The English poet Robert Browning wrote: "I was ever a fighter" and "We fall to rise, [buffeted] to fight better." I have treasured these words since I was a youth.

As you know, I have adhered to the challenging path of kosen-rufu since the age of nineteen. Over those long years, I've faced harsh and bitter times. But one who is dedicated to the mission of spreading the Mystic Law will be protected by all the benevolent forces in the universe. No way of life could be more exhilarating than this.

There is no defeat for those who practice the Mystic Law. One who is not defeated is an eternal victor, a monarch of happiness and a master of life. This is what our Buddhist faith is for, and this is why we proceed along this path. A veritable mountain of treasures and innumerable benevolent deities joyfully await all who push ahead.

As a wise champion
of kosen-rufu
upholding Buddhism,
take pride
and lead the way to victory.

I once sent this poem to a member who was struggling against adversity. He immediately responded with a letter expressing his determination, and he cited words from the Swiss philosopher Carl Hilty to the effect that people who have suffered in life only trust those who've experienced hardship themselves. His letter closed with the pledge "With that resolve, I will strive to become truly wise, sparing no effort."

Hilty himself lived a life filled with difficulties, but to a friend who visited him in his final year, he said: "If I were to erase all of the sufferings from my life, I would have no good memories left. Everything grew out of such times [of suffering]." By encountering many obstacles, a genuine leader can develop the ability to guide and encourage others. This is a principle that we should never forget.

In the words of Nichiren, "The greater the hardships befalling [the votary of the Lotus Sutra], the greater the delight he feels, because of his strong faith" (WND-1, 33). In this light, the hardships and powerful opponents that we of the men's division encounter serve to strengthen and revitalize us until our lives burn with a bright and vigorous flame.

When Hilty was asked the secret to remaining young at heart, he declared that it is always to learn something new. A life of continual learning is forever young.

The older students enrolled in Soka University's correspondence education program, studying alongside the younger students at the school, exude a splendid youthfulness and inner beauty.

The ancient Greek poet Theognis, whom I've always admired, declared: "A man who's friend in word but not in deed is not my friend . . . He must prove, if he can, by action, that he's good." My mentor, Josei Toda, was also very stern about people who were all talk and no action. On the other hand, he treasured down-to-earth, unpretentious people who made a sincere and heartfelt effort, people who worked hard and produced tangible results. He was always paying careful attention to the prayers and struggles of his disciples. It is most fortunate to have such a mentor in life.

At the September 1953 headquarters leaders meeting, Mr. Toda said, "Though you may hold a leadership position, if you don't have a challenging spirit, you won't gain benefit." He also declared: "Don't be cowardly! Cowards have neither the ability nor the qualifications to lead."

In the home, breadwinners have the mission and responsibility to protect and support the family. In an organization, in the strictest sense, everything depends upon the resolve and challenging spirit of its leaders.

In September 1953, Kamata Chapter became the first in Japan to gain more than a thousand new households in a single month. It had been a little more than a year and a half since the February campaign, when the members in Kamata and I broke through the impasse in the Soka Gakkai's propagation efforts by introducing 201 new households in one month. Suddenly, even that record had been broken in a new, golden achievement.

Kamata's greatest momentum in reaching that second landmark came from Yaguchi District, which introduced more than three hundred new households. The campaign there was led by Shigeji Shiraki, the district leader and a real pillar of support for those around him. He was later appointed as the chapter leader of Kamata, the second to hold that position. Mr. Shiraki was a company executive and a man of character and sound common sense. He showed great compassion in his concern for district members, expressing a love for them that would rival that of a parent.

In those days, the Soka Gakkai was structured as a "vertical line" organization—that is, new members, regardless of where they lived, were assigned to the group and district to which the person who introduced them belonged. Wherever his members might be struggling in Japan—be they in Akita, Hokkaido, Aichi, Gifu or Yamanashi—Mr. Shiraki would gladly visit and personally encourage them, often traveling long distances in his earnest desire to offer support.

Members felt that they could talk to him about anything, and so they fondly referred to him as "Uncle Shiraki." The tremendous respect and trust they had for him were clearly evident in the way they would call out that nickname. And when it was time to gear up for the next campaign, Mr. Shiraki would burn with the fighting spirit of an ardent youth. Those who take on challenges with a positive, upbeat attitude shine with a special brightness, irrespective of their age. And because Mr. Shiraki had this quality, he was able to foster many capable individuals.

Behind the scenes, Mr. Toda was always saying in praise, "That Shiraki, he is gaining all kinds of benefit."

Cherishing
health
and long life,
may you enjoy boundless honors
in the prime of your years.

A challenging spirit provides the energy to boldly stand at the forefront of any struggle.

Chinese Premier Zhou Enlai embodied this quality throughout his life. He once visited a dam construction site outside Beijing and spent a week there, sleeping, eating and working side by side with the laborers. More than five hundred central party leaders joined him in this effort. The premier and the other party leaders carried stones in handcarts and formed relay lines to pass stones from one person to another as they built retaining banks. Premier Zhou was already sixty years old at the time, and the average age of the party leaders with him was more than forty-five. But in spite of that, they worked "like dragons and tigers."

Moreover, after the other laborers were all sleeping, exhausted from the day's work, Premier Zhou remained awake, cutting back on his rest so he could also take care of affairs of state. The lights in his room seemingly never went out.

The brigade that Premier Zhou led was dubbed the Huang Zhong Brigade, as a sign of respect. Huang Zhong was a renowned leader under Zhuge Liang (also known as Chuko K'ung-ming) in the age of the Three Kingdoms in ancient China. Huang Zhong continued to serve as a general even though he was almost seventy years old. It is written that when he once faced an opposing general, he shouted as he rushed bravely to the attack: "Do you despise me for my age? You will find my good sword, however, young enough."

When Huang Zhong took the lead, the entire army was roused to fight. *Records of the Three Kingdoms* describes his stirring attitude in battle: "He held his halberd aloft, was always first in the attack, encouraged the foot soldiers, made the gongs and drums resound to the heavens and shook the valleys with his joyful battle cries."

The Taiyo-kai (Sun Group) and Kanto-kai (Fighting Spirit Group)—groups comprised of men's division members who have retired from their jobs and now participate in kosen-rufu activities during the day—represent the glorious Huang Zhong Brigade of the Soka Gakkai. I hope the members of these groups will take care of their health as they continue to advance in high spirits.

There is, of course, a retirement age in one's career. But there is no retirement age in a life dedicated to chanting and spreading Nam-myoho-renge-kyo, which enables us to attain eternal and indestructible victory and enjoy a life force as strong and radiant as the rising sun.

Your descendants
for generations to come
will enjoy benefits
based on the causes
made by you, their forefathers.

The citadels of our lives, built through our fierce struggles against daunting odds, are unassailable and indestructible.

Nichiren describes the vicissitudes experienced by Shakyamuni's trusted disciple Sudatta: "Seven times he became poor, and seven times he became a wealthy man" (WND-1, 1086). Rising and falling fortunes are an inescapable part of the real world. Sudatta's seventh period of poverty was especially severe, but even then, in the worst of times, he and his wife continued to follow the Buddhist teaching of striving to create good causes by assisting others. The benefits the couple reaped from such acts ensured that they rose again from the depths, becoming the richest people in the land and attaining an expansive life-state that enabled them to donate Jetavana Monastery to Shakyamuni and his followers. In praising Sudatta and his wife for the victory they achieved by striving in faith with the same spirit as Shakyamuni, Nichiren states, "From this, you should understand all things" (WND-1, 1086).

Buddhism teaches the Law of cause and effect that allows us to accumulate inexhaustible benefits. The Buddhist scriptures also describe the Buddha as one who is "supreme in the spiritual realm," having the power to "vanquish demons" (see *Gosho zenshu*, 818). Summon forth this power of the Buddha! Vanquish all devilish, negative influences and win in all areas of your life. And, while supporting the women and young women, do your best, inspire others through your dauntless courage and win the trust of those in your workplace and community.

N. Radhakrishnan, a leading Gandhian scholar, is a good friend of mine. His father, Neelakanta Pillai, worked alongside Mahatma Gandhi in the nonviolent struggle for Indian independence and was known for his fearlessness and utter lack of concern for social status, power or wealth. Dr. Radhakrishnan was told by his mentor G. Ramachandran that, as the courageous son of his great father, he should also strive his utmost to become a man of character and a victor in life. The most precious legacy one can leave one's children and juniors is a triumphant record of achievements, attained by remaining true to one's convictions.

Napoleon Bonaparte summed up the essence of successful leadership, declaring that the key to victory is the individual, not the number of individuals involved. The victory of kosen-rufu also depends entirely on each individual. For a member of the men's division, his greatest source of pride is the number of victories he has achieved through faith.

It's not about others; it's about you. It's about you winning and winning over yourself. By doing so, you will provide inspiration and encouragement to all.

Like phoenixes,
inseparable as life and its environment,
you and I.

I composed this poem on August 24, 1977, the thirtieth anniversary of the day I joined the Soka Gakkai. It was also Men's Division Day. I was calling upon all the trusted members of the men's division to advance, together with me, like phoenixes arising from the ashes. The phrase "inseparable as life and its environment" refers to the profound Buddhist teaching that living beings, the initiators of action, are one with their environment, the place where that action unfolds.

We employ the strategy of the Lotus Sutra to triumph over inconceivably arduous circumstances and build strong selves that cannot be shaken by anything. As we win and win again, we are at the same time creating an environment of the most resplendent success and glory. In all things, life and environment are one. Therefore, by achieving self-mastery, we also achieve victory in our environment.

Nichiren wrote to the Ikegami brothers, who can be considered precursors of the men's division, "You must grit your teeth and never slacken in your faith" (WND-1, 498). He also encouraged them to be as fearless as he had been when he confronted the powerful government official Hei no Saemon and boldly spoke out to refute the erroneous and reveal the true.

Men's division members who share the same commitment in faith as their mentor strive in the spirit of champions. Disciples, advance bravely along the great path to victory that your mentor has opened for you!

When the French government's "Mona Lisa" exhibition was held in Japan in 1974 [at the Tokyo National Museum], it was accompanied by a special representative, the French writer and art critic André Malraux. At that time, we met at the Seikyo Shimbun Building in Shinanomachi, Tokyo, and conversed for nearly three hours. In May 1975, he invited me to his home on the outskirts of Paris. There, we talked about many subjects, including the future of culture and civilization in general.

Mr. Malraux said one thing that seemed to me to summarize his personal philosophy: "Do what you believe you must and leave the interpreting of it to others." How true this is. Don't be distracted by the carping of bystanders, their irresponsible attitudes, their self-serving, cowardly words and actions. We are champions of kosen-rufu, undying as phoenixes. We share an everlasting vow as mentor and disciple and a supreme mission from time without beginning. Our challenge lies ahead, and it is imperative that we succeed. There is no trail we cannot blaze, no wall we cannot topple, no struggle we cannot win. So let's get to it!

And let's win, completely and utterly, so that we may leave a profound and magnificent record of achievement for our descendants and all future generations. Let's live out our lives as great actors playing the role of courageous human beings on the eternal stage of life. My precious fellow men's division members, my inseparable comrades in faith walking life's most noble path—never forget for an instant that the heavenly deities are cheering you on; they are protecting you now and will protect you always.

As men rich in happiness
sharing the same spirit
as your mentor,
strive courageously
like lions
and win victory after victory.

POEM

The Great Citadel of Resounding Victory

— COMMEMORATING AUG. 24, SGI MEN'S DIVISION DAY

By Shin'ichi Yamamoto
[the name SGI President Ikeda uses for his character in
The Human Revolution *and* The New Human Revolution]

A new century
Dawns.
A new age
Begins.
Champions of fresh construction
Rise to action.

We
Climb the mountain of peace
And supreme happiness.
Stirring trumpets
Sound a glorious paean
In praise of peace,
In praise of life's majesty.

My friends who have lost
A beloved wife!
My friends who have lost
A beloved child!
And also
My friends who have fallen ill
And are battling valiantly against
their illness!

My friends, noble emissaries of the Buddha!
Knowing that patience is compassion,
You continue to strive selflessly for kosen-rufu
Amid your own hardships and sufferings.

Each of you
Has a mission.
Each of you
Has a track record
Of victory.

Please etch deep in your heart
The fact that I am always with you
As your true comrade in faith!

Transcending the age of hatred,
Let us together exercise our talent
For setting an example for the world
By presenting an actual framework
For a new culture
In the new century!

Dismantling the internal elements
Of the immature culture
That has led humanity to war,
Let us together build
A magnificent new culture
Based on lofty ideals
That spring from a life-affirming
philosophy!

In so doing,
We may face a series
Of tense struggles
Unprecedented in scale.

But
No matter how people
With base and malicious hearts
May try to crush us,
Our fair and just spirit
Will never waver.

The more
Our enemies
Attack us,
The more our lives are infused
With invincible spirit,
Burning stronger and higher;
The more certain it is
That our brilliant struggle
Will be adorned in resounding victory.

My mentor, Josei Toda,
Frequently said to me:
"Benefits come naturally
After waging a struggle for the Law.
It is foolish and unreasonable
To expect them beforehand."

And only after you have triumphed
Through bitter struggles,
Will the satisfaction
Of victory shine
And enfold your life in its radiant light.

My friends,
You must not
Make this life
You were born into
Meaningless.

A crown alone
Does not make one a monarch.
Only when you yourself
Fight and win
Will you be accorded the crown
Of a champion in life.

My friends,
Never let yourselves be dragged away
To the gallows of defeat,
Think of the raging waves of persecution
As but an instant on the way
To great and magnificent happiness!

My friends!
My friends!
Do not lead sad lives
Bereft of joy and vitality!

Do not be swayed
By the unfounded criticisms of society,
But know
That every accolade
Adorns your life with unsurpassed honor
As bright as the shining sun.

We are entities of the Mystic Law!
No matter how
Spiteful criticism
May swirl around us,
No matter how
Malodorous attacks
May try to rend our spirit,
Our commitment to justice and truth
Remains steadfast.

We shine brilliantly,
As we make our way undefeated
Through this human realm
Pervaded by immense darkness.
We will leave behind
A beautiful memory free of regret
For the eternal future.

My friends,
Let us win without fail!
We must win without fail!

Though your line of work
May be filled with difficult challenges,
Do not let them defeat you!
Though you may encounter
Deranged attacks,
Do not be afraid!

Mirthless and terrible,
The evil
Cannot survive
In a pure world of hopes and dreams
Under the serene light of the full moon.

Illuminated by that moon,
Hearts open wide,
Giving voice to our souls,
And performing a great symphony
Of joy and hope,
We return
To our eternal great citadel,
Step by step,
Bright,
Brave and positive,
And filled with jubilation.

What were we born
Into this world
To accomplish?
What is the purpose
Of our appearance
In this world?

When we say farewell
To this world,
Our great lives of mission
Will close in brilliant splendor
Brighter than the brightest sun,
Bringing hope and inspiration to all.

No matter how the years may pass,
Do not forget to stay young at heart!
Never grow old in spirit!
Always remember
That herein lies
The secret to eternal youth
Free of regrets.

The rulings of cause and effect
Are fair and impartial above all.

Let us arise!
Indeed,
We must arise!
We must advance
And fight!
And
We must win!

My friends,
From your hearts
Cast out the word *fear*,
Erase the word *cowardice*,
Banish the word *despair*!

The Ukrainian poet
Lesya Ukrainka said:
"What is there to be gained
By crying over this
Persecution-rife world?
We cannot afford to back down.
Therefore, we must fight!
We must realize a bright new age."

Today, again,
The sun shines brightly
Above your heads,
Protecting and illuminating you
As if you were precious gems.

My friends,
With firm determination
And deep prayer,
Live and fight
To the end,
Until you can behold
The gratifying banner of victory
That lies on the far side
Of a fierce struggle.

Our struggle
Is not one
Merely to enable us
To enjoy our lives today.
It is a struggle
To enable us
To enjoy our lives for many ages to come—
No,
For all eternity.

You have endured.
I have endured.
You have won.
I have won.
You have no regrets.
I have no regrets.

The lives
Of we who live out
This human existence together,
Sharing
Supreme fulfillment
And infinite value,
Are everlasting.

This is
The Law of Buddhism,
An ironclad principle.

Therefore,
When it is time for us
To be reborn again,
Let us be reborn together.
Let us strive and
Win together,
And again adorn
Another act
In the drama of our eternal lives
In victory.
Let us win
And shake hands firmly,
Celebrating our triumph!

A new, glorious advance
Has once again
Begun!

—With my prayers for your successful endeavors, happiness and longevity. Praise to the men's division in each country!

AUGUST 14, 2001

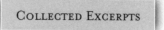

Faith Equals Courage

From the July 16, 2009, speech

When a men's division member stands up, he can lead a thousand.

The Brazilian writer and journalist Fernando Sabino declared to the effect that victory is always preceded by interruptions and obstacles and that such setbacks should be regarded as opportunities for new breakthroughs. I'd like to present this message to the youth division. My young friends, I entrust everything to you!

Thank you also to the men's division members for all your efforts! No matter how old you are, always be sure to speak with a youthful energetic voice. Men face many challenges, it's true. At work, your younger colleagues will have nothing to do with you, and then when you come home, you're scolded by your wife and criticized by your daughter! That's what I hear from a lot of men, anyway. *[Laughter.]*

Members of the men's division, make your way proudly and in high spirits, like victorious generals! Strive with all your might alongside the youth. Those who do so brim with youthfulness and joy.

Now is the time for the men's division to earnestly rise into action. Advance toward the eightieth anniversary of the Soka Gakkai's founding [in 2010] with "absolute victory" as your motto. In a family, too, there's no limit to what can be achieved when everyone lends a hand. It's only natural that the youth are active and full of energy, but if the men's division members can join them in that spirit, the Soka Gakkai will be able to display double, triple or still many times the strength that it has in the past. Please bear this deeply in mind.

You, the members of the men's division, mustn't allow yourselves to grow old in spirit. Don't let your faith stagnate. Be youthful and continue to win in society. I really want to encourage you.

The members of the women's division, the suns of kosen-rufu, are cheerfully making energetic efforts. The young men are striding forward powerfully, and the young women are sparkling—indeed, the youth division as a whole is doing an excellent job. Now, the men's division is crucial, because when a men's division member gives his all, he can lead a thousand along with him. Final victory rests with the men's division. Make this your focus.

Just like the unstoppable momentum of the Amazon, win victory after victory.

The Brazilian author João Guimarães Rosa wrote, "All rivers are new." This is a simple but profound statement. The same is true of the river of the heart. I pray sincerely that the Federal University of Rondônia will continue to grow and develop with all the dynamism and power of the Amazon River, mighty and ever new.

Let's all make a firm resolve today to forge ahead intrepidly, winning victory after victory, with just the same invincible, unstoppable momentum as the Amazon, that most majestic of rivers.

(August 14, 2009, World Tribune, *p. 5)*

FROM THE SERIES

The Hope-filled Teachings of Nichiren Daishonin

[In his letter "A Warning against Begrudging One's Fief," Nichiren] unstintingly commends Kingo for his staunch faith, because it is extremely rare for an ordinary person in the evil age of the Latter Day to undertake the difficult challenge of maintaining faith in the Lotus Sutra and standing up for kosen-rufu.

This challenge is so difficult because remaining steadfast in faith means battling the ignorance or darkness in the depths of our lives—in other words, making continuous efforts to transform our lives on a fundamental level. This is an extremely arduous path because those who pursue it are certain to be assailed by the three obstacles and four devils, along with the three powerful enemies. However, we can only truly attain Buddhahood by defeating these obstacles and steadfastly working on our inner transformation. Nichiren no doubt praised Kingo because the latter had struggled alongside him as a great pioneer on the path of "attaining Buddhahood as an ordinary person" in the Latter Day of the Law . . .

Devilish functions seek to bring down the "pillars," or the mainstays, of the Buddhist community of believers. This is precisely why such people must stand firm. In particular, the members of the men's division—the golden pillars of kosen-rufu—have a mission to secure the path established by the Daishonin and carry through with faith that would win his praise, just as their great predecessor, Shijo Kingo, had.

In many writings, the Daishonin guides and encourages Kingo, a key figure among his followers, to live out his life as a worthy or sage. In this present letter, too, he tells him: "It is the nature of ordinary people not to know what awaits them in the future. Those who have a full understanding of this are called worthies or sages" (WND-1, 824).

To not know what will happen to us in the future is our lot as ordinary people. However, by maintaining faith in the Mystic Law, we can make our way through life as worthies or sages based on the Buddhist wisdom that we can tap from within. President Toda said that we can develop the life-state of "an ordinary person enlightened from time without beginning." This is because faith in the Mystic Law enables us to draw forth from the depths of our lives fundamental wisdom equal to that of the Buddha.

(September–October 2009 Living Buddhism, *pp. 77–79)*

From the November 14, 2009, speech

Lead Vibrant, Victorious Lives

The report from the International Group members featured a number of inspiring words from Mahatma Gandhi. They had found them in the course of their reading and felt they might be encouraging for the men's division members who were working very hard in their local organizations. Allow me now to share some of these words with you.

Gandhi wrote: "Manliness consists in struggling. It is such struggling that molds us. Hence be fearless and fight on. Never lose heart, and, if [you are thrown] down, though you may have fought with all your strength, do not get dejected in the least. Be on your feet again and resume the fight."

I was deeply moved by the sincere spirit of these International Group members who searched out these passages for me, and impressed by their diligence in studying the writings of Gandhi, a great champion of nonviolence.

Gandhi also said: "All of us . . . can cultivate virtues like fearlessness, truthfulness, fortitude, justice, straightforwardness, firmness of purpose and dedicate them to the service of the nation. This is the religious way." Our members who are contributing to their respective communities and countries as good citizens embody just this religious way of which Gandhi speaks.

Gandhi further stated: "If we would but learn the lessons that have to be learned from our adversity, it will not have been lost upon us. We would emerge from the trial a community richer in social virtues, stronger in the justice of our cause." If we're always just having a good time, laughing and enjoying ourselves, never experiencing any suffering or hardship, we will not be able to gain anything truly profound or meaningful. It is adversity and challenge that develop character.

I especially call on our men's division members to use adversity as a springboard and once again rise vigorously into action.

(December 18, 2009, World Tribune, p. 5)

Concerned for the safety of Shijo Kingo, Nichiren repeatedly warned him to be careful and prudent: "Be millions of times more careful than ever" (WND-1, 839); "Maintain a strict guard at night" (WND-2, 731).

Second Soka Gakkai president Josei Toda also urged the members of the women's and young women's divisions time and time again not to get home too late at night or to walk down dark streets alone. Our women's and young women's division members should take care that their evening meetings finish at a reasonable hour so they can get home safely. I can't stress this enough.

I hope that each of you will wisely take responsibility for your own safety and well-being, making your way as champions of health and happiness.

By the same token, I hope that our male leaders in particular will always remain alert and attentive to the importance of ensuring the safety of our female members . . .

It's time now for the members of the young men's division and the men's division, as well as the top leaders of our organization, to stand up with fresh energy and commitment.

Leaders who lose the spirit of taking personal responsibility for kosen-rufu no longer qualify to lead. Those in leadership positions who shun hard work and only think about their own interests won't be able to savor the true joy of Buddhist practice.

The great path of kosen-rufu has been opened by each of us awakening to our mission and standing up to respond to the call of our mentor.

(December 25, 2009, World Tribune, p. 6)

Charge Ahead Like Lions

I HOPE THE MEMBERS OF OUR MEN'S and young men's divisions will always behave like gentlemen toward the members of the women's and young women's divisions. Please never be arrogant or domineering. Soka women are worthy of the highest respect. None are working harder for kosen-rufu than they. It is completely unacceptable to make light of their efforts or treat them in a disrespectful way. That is the behavior of the lowest of the low. Gentlemen always follow the rule of "ladies first." Any other behavior is not acceptable in the Soka Gakkai.

There are base and malicious people in society. That is the kind of reality in which we are carrying out our efforts for kosen-rufu, a struggle to bring about a fundamental transformation in the depths of people's lives. There may be times when enduring their negativity or criticism may seem too hard or off-putting. I understand. But you mustn't give up. Just bravely carry on, steadily surmounting each obstacle or challenge. That's the way to attain inner victory. Please never forget that.

(June 5, 2009, World Tribune, pp. 4–5)

Creating a Glorious History With the Youth

I'D ALSO LIKE TO THANK THE MEMBERS of the men's division, the golden pillars of kosen-rufu and society. The men's division is very important. You're all so youthful! That's great. In Japan today, the number of young people is declining. We should advance with the firm determination that the men's division is the new young men's division. Men who understand that and exude a youthful spirit can triumph. Organizations and countries alike can continue to succeed and prosper when they maintain a youthful spirit. When someone asks how old you are, just subtract thirty from your age before you answer! *[Laughter]* Of course, women will have to be on the alert for this trick! *[Laughter]*

(*March 27, 2009,* World Tribune, *pp. 4–5)*

FROM THE MAY 27, 2009, SPEECH

Decide, Chant and Take Action

MY FRIENDS IN THE MEN'S and young men's divisions, let's all stand up and express our appreciation to the women's division!

Men and women are equally respectworthy. Nichiren proclaims: "There should be no discrimination among those who propagate the five characters of Myoho-renge-kyo in the Latter Day of the Law, be they men or women" (WND-1, 385). I've always highly valued the members of the women's and young women's divisions.

We need to treasure those who are working hard to further our movement for kosen-rufu, those who are sincerely sharing Nichiren Buddhism with others and offering wholehearted encouragement and guidance in faith to fellow members.

Criticizing or harassing those who are doing their best for positive aims cannot be described as humanistic behavior. Such actions are unforgivable. The arrogance of domineering individuals needs to be severely rebuked.

Please remember also that true gentlemen are always kind to women.

(*June 26, 2009,* World Tribune, *p. 5)*

FROM THE JUNE 16, 2009, SPEECH

Strive With Courage

MEN'S LEADERS SHOULD ALWAYS wholeheartedly praise and commend the members of the women's and young women's divisions for their noble endeavors. It is absolutely unforgivable if there should be leaders who scold women or treat them in a domineering fashion. Second Soka Gakkai president Josei Toda was quite strict on this point. To always protect and treasure women—this is the epitome of proper conduct for men and an expression of sterling character; it is the chivalrous spirit of knights.

(July 10, 2009, World Tribune, *p. 4)*

The members of the women's and young women's divisions are cheerfully promoting friendship and steadfastly opening the way to victory, undaunted by any obstacle. The men in our organization should sincerely respect and wholeheartedly support our dedicated women's division members who are striving very hard for kosen-rufu. When this spirit is alive, true unity is possible. This spirit is a sign of genuine character and integrity. Men, I'm counting on you!

(July 17, 2009, World Tribune, *p. 4)*

FROM THE DECEMBER 13, 2008, SPEECH

Through Struggles, an Unshakable Self

IN THE PAST TURBULENT YEAR, how immeasurably the smiles of Soka women—the mothers of kosen-rufu—have brightened the times and cheered and encouraged everyone! Let's express our deepest appreciation to them. I'd like all the men in the audience to stand up and convey their respect and gratitude to our women's division members. Members of the women's division, thank you very much for everything! [The men in the audience do so, and everyone applauds.]

No matter how self-importantly male leaders may behave or make a show of their authority, it is undeniably the women's division members who are really advancing our movement for kosen-rufu. No one can match their tireless, dedicated, grassroots efforts in talking to others about Nichiren Buddhism or making friends in the community. The women's division also leads the way in offering sincere and thoughtful personal guidance to members.

Men must never behave in an arrogant or domineering fashion to the women in our organization who are working so hard for kosen-rufu. Scolding and berating these dedicated members is absolutely out of the question. The way to great development and victory lies in our organization always highly valuing and appreciating the women and young women who are striving wholeheartedly for the sake of Buddhism, the members and the Soka Gakkai.

(*January 30, 2009,* World Tribune, *p. 4*)

FROM THE MARCH 7, 2007, SPEECH

Win With Courage, Perseverance and Unity!

CONGRATULATIONS ALSO ON THE men's division leaders meeting today. In a letter encouraging Toki Jonin's wife, Myojo, who was battling illness, Nichiren mentions Shijo Kingo, writing: "You can go to Nakatsukasa Saburo Saemon-no-jo [Shijo Kingo], who is not only an excellent physician but a votary of the Lotus Sutra . . . He is a man who never gives in to defeat and who greatly values his friends" (WND-1, 955).

Our stalwart men's division members, especially those in the doctors division, are modern-day Shijo Kingos. With their indomitable

spirit, they valiantly support and protect their fellow members and help guide them to victory. This is the essence of the men's division. When the men's division is strong and active, the women's division is happy, and the youth division can grow and develop. I call on all our men's division members to stand up vigorously like Shijo Kingo.
(March 30, 2007, World Tribune, p. 2)

In another scene in *The Iliad,* a warrior calls on others to show valor, urging them, "My friends . . . keep a stout heart!" Second Soka Gakkai president Josei Toda often used to put his arm around the shoulders of men's or young men's division members and urge them to act with courage and determination. I, too, call on all the members of the men's division, the young men's division and the young men's student division to exert themselves with courage and determination.
(April 13, 2007, World Tribune, p. 2)

FROM THE JANUARY 6, 2007, SPEECH

You Can Move Everything In a Positive Direction

NICHIREN WRITES, "THERE SHOULD BE NO discrimination among those who propagate the five characters of Myoho-renge-kyo in the Latter Day of the Law, be they men or women" (WND-1, 385). This is a great declaration of gender equality. Given this, it's unacceptable for any male leader of our organization to look down on women or arrogantly order them about. Unless we can eliminate such attitudes and behavior, the Soka Gakkai's growth will come to a standstill.

Mr. Toda said: "Ordinary men and women, the dedicated, regular members, are the most trustworthy people. Women, like our

Soka women's division members, always remain unfazed in a crisis. They are courageous and fearless. You need to look to and follow their example. Never forget their courage. Always make them your model. You should show the highest respect to these true champions!"

Ordinary people are the most important. And it is the earnest struggles of great Soka women who have made the Soka Gakkai what it is today. You must never forget this, not even for a fleeting moment. Men, in particular, have a tendency to grow arrogant and succumb to corrupting influences when they rise to high leadership positions in an organization or gain prominence in society. I am determined to speak out frankly and say what must be said to prevent that.

To our top male leaders in the Soka Gakkai: Please greet our women's division and young women's division members with a smile, always thanking them for their efforts and treating them courteously and with the utmost respect. You should pledge to work hard alongside them. Please make these true champions, the Soka women, your ideal and model. That was Mr. Toda's stern request.

If the Soka Gakkai genuinely respects women, it will grow and develop to many times its present size. This is the Age of Women. The Soka Gakkai must not be left behind. I call on all our men's division and young men's division members to engrave this point in their hearts.

(February 9, 2007, *World Tribune*, p. 2)

FROM THE MARCH 9, 2006, SPEECH

A Revolution In One Person Inspires Others

NICHIREN STATES QUITE PLAINLY, "A woman who embraces this sutra not only excels all other women, but also surpasses all men"

(WND-1, 464). I have shared this passage with you on numerous occasions. In light of Nichiren's writings, it is wrong for any man to look down on or behave in a domineering fashion toward women who work for kosen-rufu. Such an attitude is also undemocratic, feudal and hopelessly outdated. Women tend to be serious and pure-hearted. They have a strong sense of right and wrong. The future of the Soka Gakkai will be in peril if men regard women as a nuisance and insist on leaving the decision making to men alone. This can cause great turmoil and even the destruction of our organization.

One important key to our eternal development as an organization is whether men can sincerely and truly respect women. I am fighting to open up a century of women and bring an end to the deeply rooted sexism that is particularly prevalent here in Japan.

Unity among leaders is also crucial. If leaders aren't in close communication and on good terms with one another, then they are creating an opening for devilish functions to enter and erode the organization. Please always advance in the spirit of "many in body, one in mind."

Congratulations on the fortieth anniversary of the men's division. [The division was established on March 5, 1966.] I hope that each of you, brimming with ever-greater vigor and vitality, will continue to compassionately foster young people while expanding your own life-condition. To commemorate this occasion, I'll share with you some words from the great liberator of Latin America, Simón Bolívar.

"Without strength, there is no virtue," declared Bolívar. The weak cannot remain virtuous. Only those who are strong can shine with goodness and justice. "Strong" in this context does not mean "domineering." Bolívar is talking about moral strength, the strength to work for good.

He also said, "Glory lies not in giving orders, but in the practice of great virtue." This is certainly true.

Bolívar further insisted, "Leaders must listen to the opinions of others, no matter how painful the truth may be." Please make a special effort to listen to the opinions of the women and young women members.

Strength, dedication and big-heartedness are the requirements of leaders and inspiring leadership, and these qualities are only going to be in greater demand from now on.

Bolívar also declared, "I have a thousand times more trust in the nation's people than in their [political leaders]." The people come first. Members come first. Never, ever forget this.

It has been, and always should be, the role of all men's division members to protect their fellow members and lead the way to victory after victory.

I'm a men's division member, too, and I will exert myself even harder for kosen-rufu. With the energy and force of a swooping eagle, I will boldly fight on all fronts—to open a new age and to protect the welfare of all our members around the world.

(March 31, 2006, World Tribune, *p. 1)*

FROM THE OCTOBER 13, 2005, SPEECH

Challenges Lead to a Vibrant Life

I HOPE THE MEN'S DIVISION WILL STAND UP with as much vigor as the women's division. Please take pride in the fact that your hard work has contributed so greatly to the Soka Gakkai's development and the country's prosperity. This time of your lives is not a twilight period of inexorable decline. The Daishonin assures us that those who uphold the Mystic Law grow younger and accumulate more good fortune with each passing year (see WND-1, 464).

I hope that Soka men will become more robust and vigorous as they accumulate years and experience in life. Victory in life is not decided halfway through our journey but in the final few years. The purpose of our faith is to enable us to shine at that time with the brilliant golden light of a magnificently setting sun. Let us devote ourselves to kosen-rufu to the very end so that we can adorn the closing chapters of our existence in this world with the courage, confidence and freedom of true champions of life. Let's do our best!

(November 11, 2005, World Tribune, *p. 1)*

FROM THE ESSAY

There Is No Retirement in Faith

YOUR CHILDREN MAY BE GROWN UP and you may have grandchildren. Your living situation may be secure. But if you rest on your laurels, you run the risk of endangering the brilliant closing chapter of life that should be yours. Smugness about your past achievements, the fear of tackling new challenges, a feeling of reserve around young people—all of these are openings that can invite old age to set up house in your heart.

The person who continues striving to the very end is truly admirable, genuinely young at heart, eternally ageless and a victor whose life is replete with the greatest happiness and fulfillment.

If you lose your fighting spirit, you can be old at fifty, but if you are still moving forward with enthusiasm, you can be young at eighty.

(January 28, 2005, Seikyo Shimbun; *SGI-USA Publications 1997–2008 CD,* Bonus Articles*)*

FROM THE JULY 30, 2004, SPEECH

Attain the Unchanging Spirit of a Champion

I CALL ON YOU TO ADVANCE IN HIGH SPIRITS and win through all with outstanding leadership like that demonstrated by Chuko K'ung-ming [or Zhuge Liang, the famous Chinese military strategist and prime minister].

And male leaders—particularly the leaders of the men's division—need to make even more earnest and sincere efforts and show the highest respect toward our women and young women. Any organization that fails to value women is bound to be left behind and fall into decline. I say this again and again because it is so important for our male leaders to take this truth deeply to heart.

It is important to keep moving forward.

(September 24, 2004, World Tribune, p. 1)

FROM THE AUGUST 3, 2003, SPEECH

Kosen-rufu Will Advance to the Same Degree That Leaders Grow

NO NEW VALUE CAN BE CREATED if we stay rigidly attached to how things have been done in the past. Leaders must constantly ask themselves: "How can we move forward? What can we do, so that everyone can advance with enthusiasm and fresh hope?"

One important key to achieving this, I believe, is for men to take greater initiative and set a shining example for everyone. The women's division is a crucial force in our organization, serving as the mainstay of our Gakkai activities. It is, therefore, vital that men, and in particular the men's division, likewise rise to action and devote themselves to kosen-rufu in earnest.

Each of us must start by challenging ourselves. It may seem like a simple thing, but if each of us does this, it will set in motion a momentous wave of change. Let us challenge ourselves anew now.

It is also important to clarify goals and responsibilities. These, too, of course, must not be forced on others. Also, people will not feel motivated to make a genuine effort if such things are conveyed to them in a mechanical or bureaucratic manner. We need to communicate our spirit. We need to touch others' hearts and inspire them.

(Embracing Compassion, *vol. 1, p. 59)*

FROM THE ESSAY

The Fundamental Power To Transform Our Lives

IT IS THE MISSION AND RESPONSIBILITY of the top leaders of our organization to work selflessly and wholeheartedly for the sake of their fellow members and the Law.

I especially hope the men's division leaders will make up for what they may lack in physical stamina with brain power and decisive leadership that will pave the way to victory. I ask that they give constant thought to what they can do to make it easier for everyone to carry out their activities, what they can do to inspire everyone with enthusiasm and joy. And that they also take concrete measures toward that end.

(June 29, 2001, *World Tribune*, p. 5)

COLLECTED POEMS

THE FOLLOWING POEMS COMMEMORATE
MAY 3, 2007, SOKA GAKKAI DAY

DEDICATED TO THE MEN'S DIVISION:

Boldly advancing
and winning
in rhythm with
kosen-rufu,
carry out your great
mission
to lead the way to victory.

ojo

Resolutely score
a glorious triumph
and secure perfect
victory.

(June 1, 2007, World Tribune, *p. 3)*

DEDICATED TO THE MEN'S DIVISION

Please take care of yourselves
so that you may enjoy long lives
and good health.
May the prime of your lives
be filled with success and honor.

How joyous—
you are healthy,
and I am, too!
Please adorn your lives
with immeasurable value.

(January 19, 2007, World Tribune, *p. 3)*

DEDICATED TO THE MEN'S DIVISION:

Holding high
the sword of good health
and longevity,
achieve victory after victory
throughout eternity.

(June 2003 Living Buddhism, *p. 3)*

**THE FOLLOWING POEMS COMMEMORATE
MAY 3, 1997, SOKA GAKKAI DAY.**

DEDICATED TO THE MEN'S DIVISION:

Forget not for a moment
The strict love and affection
With which our late mentor cried,
"Bemoan not, my friends,
Tribulation however great!"

Wherever the great procession
Of the SGI advances
Unfolds an Eagle Peak
Alive with a profusion
Of untold fragrant flowers

❧

Since we faithfully
Practice his sacred teachings
The Daishonin surely
Rejoices and delights
Embracing us as his children

(June 13, 1997, World Tribune, *p. 13)*

EXCERPTS

The New Human Revolution

SECURING THE FOUNDATION

AFTER SIGHTSEEING, Shin'ichi headed for Ryuan-ji, the temple where the men's division group leaders meeting was to be held. It had been built and donated to Nichiren Shoshu by the Soka Gakkai in December 1959, when there were only a few members living in the Amami Islands. Believing it would be a great source of strength for future kosen-rufu activities, Shin'ichi had proposed its establishment. The Soka Gakkai had always given the construction of temples and the growth of Nichiren Shoshu top priority, even if it meant delaying the construction of Soka Gakkai facilities.

However, the priesthood later took advantage of the Soka Gakkai's sincerity and, intending to exploit the membership, excommunicated Shin'ichi, their staunchest supporter, setting into motion a contemptible plot to disband the organization. The offense committed by these priests will never be erased.

Thus, decades after its establishment, Ryuan-ji became a stronghold for the attempted destruction of Nichiren Daishonin's Buddhism in the Amami Islands. Such malice is like a cancer. The longer it is left untreated, the farther it will spread, until it finally destroys life. That is why it is so important to challenge injustice and wrongdoing. It is the only way to protect the realm of good and to secure the correct path of faith.

At the men's division group leaders meeting, Shin'ichi spoke of the sense of commitment and responsibility required of leaders. He was profoundly aware of the hardships faced by the inhabitants of the

Amami Islands, and he knew how difficult it was for the members there to do Soka Gakkai activities. Yet, without the continuous spread of the Daishonin's teachings, the fate of Amami would not be changed and happiness for the people could not be realized. That is why Shin'ichi chose to talk about the attitude of those taking the lead in activities for kosen-rufu.

"Thank you for all your hard work every day. The challenges you face geographically, economically, and in trying to share the Daishonin's Buddhism amid deep-seated local traditions must be overwhelming. As you know, the Daishonin states that we 'voluntarily choose to be born in evil circumstances so that we may help others' (WND-1, 243). In other words, we deliberately made the negative causes that destined us to be born into this defiled age so that we could help all living beings become truly happy.

"Buddhism teaches that we appeared in the Latter Day of the Law to propagate the Daishonin's Buddhism as Bodhisattvas of the Earth. This means that all of you volunteered to be born here in the Amami Islands. Well aware that this place is frequently struck by typhoons, has poisonous snakes, is difficult to get around and suffers economically, you accepted the karmic burden and appeared here as Bodhisattvas of the Earth with a vow to work for kosen-rufu.

"If you are complaining that these circumstances are not what you expected, that they are more than you bargained for, then you are not yet demonstrating the real essence of your mission. You will in that case be unable to manifest your innate power and wisdom, which means you will not break through your problems. Only when you have a firm awareness of your mission to accomplish kosen-rufu are you a true Bodhisattva of the Earth. Then, as you strive to fulfill your mission, your eternal self will take over and boundless strength and wisdom will well forth, enabling you to surmount all obstacles."

The men's division group leaders listened intently as Shin'ichi spoke. Looking directly at each person, he continued: "Today I would like to talk about what will prevent our achievement of kosen-rufu. It is not the harshness of our circumstances or our environment, but the complacency of leaders and their willingness to give up. When leaders start thinking: 'My area has accomplished so much. There is nothing more we can do,' or 'We set a goal, but if we can't reach it, then so be it,' then they have already lost the battle.

"A strong determination is the driving force for victory. If that is lost, defeat is the only option."

(vol. 8, p. 76)

Winds of Happiness

[At a photography session for men's division group leaders in Kansai, Shin'ichi Yamamoto said:] "I want to say that I hope you will all live long and chant abundantly throughout your lives.

"In particular, I want to encourage those of you facing serious difficulties to pray to the Gohonzon earnestly and diligently, chanting Nam-myoho-renge-kyo five hundred thousand, one million or two million times to overcome them. The Gohonzon is the embodiment of the great fundamental Law of the universe. There is no reason that our problems should go unresolved. Life is full of difficulties, but if we let our problems get the better of us, it is because of our inner weaknesses.

"I am determined to open the way forward so that your children will freely take action in all fields of endeavor toward the realization of peace for Japan and the entire world. The future is secured. Please rest assured and do your absolute best."

(vol. 10, p. 149)

Heart and Soul

[At a photography session for men's division leaders in Shinjuku, Shin'ichi Yamamoto said:] "The valuable experience you have gained during your many years of dedication to kosen-rufu is a priceless treasure. I would like you to continue accumulating rich experience so that you can pass it on to the next generation.

"Some of you may think that you have nothing worth sharing with others. If that's the case, then now is the time to set personal goals and begin a new struggle, doing your utmost to contribute to kosen-rufu. There's no point in regretting the past. Buddhism focuses on the present and the future. Everything starts from today. The important thing is to courageously take action. Nothing is too late in faith.

"Men's division members tend not to throw themselves single-mindedly into things because they let their pride get in the way and think it's no use trying, or they simply can't be bothered. But such a mind-set ages your spirit. Courage is the key to break free of this. Courage connects you with your youthfulness. At any rate, your own experiences, what you achieve through your own efforts, are the real gems of your life. The French philosopher Jean-Jacques Rousseau said, 'The man who has lived the most is not he who has counted the most years but he who has most felt life'" (*Emile, or On Education*, translated by Allan Bloom [London: Penguin Books, 1991], p. 42).

(vol. 16, p. 35)

Faith Is the Ultimate Source of Victory

AUGUST 2009: FOR THE SGI-USA
MEN'S COMMEMORATIVE MEETINGS

To MY TRUSTED MEMBERS of the men's division of the SGI-USA! I extend my sincerest congratulations on holding your general meeting along with your August discussion meeting, joined by the jubilant members of the women's division and the spirited youth division.

Feeling as if I were there with you, I am watching over these gatherings of the golden pillars of kosen-rufu as they unfold harmoniously, brightly, cheerfully and amiably across the vast land of America.

You, the members of the men's division, are chanting Nam-myoho-renge-kyo resoundingly and advancing dauntlessly through the most difficult hardships during this time of great change in society. Nothing makes me happier than seeing your examples of courage and victory. I am praying with all my heart that your general meeting will be a most meaningful family event.

In a letter he wrote while in Izu, the location of his first exile, Nichiren Daishonin states, "The Buddha is also called 'One Who Can Endure'" (WND-1, 41). A victorious person is one who can persevere no matter what may happen. Everyone inevitably experiences difficulties in the course of life.

Happiness does not mean that we don't have problems. True happiness lies in having the strength to bear any hardship and overcome it. Faith is the ultimate source of genuine happiness and victory.

Your existence, which is devoted to courageously fulfilling your mission for kosen-rufu, is precious. The Buddhas and bodhisattvas of the three existences and ten directions will certainly protect your noble life. With this conviction, whatever may happen, please live determinedly, cheerfully and courageously. My earnest wish is that each of you will walk the path of triumph, and persevere to show actual proof in society.

SGI members in 192 countries and territories look to the SGI-USA as a vital example. This means that the SGI-USA men's division is the driving force for the progress of worldwide kosen-rufu. I say to you, my friends of the men's division, "Let's subtract thirty years from our actual age and advance together youthfully and vibrantly!"

You are my treasured American comrades. Along with my wife, I am earnestly praying for your good health and long lives, and the happiness of your families. Please convey our warmest regards to your family members.

SGI-USA men's division members, arise together with us and win, win again and keep winning! Cheers to the SGI-USA men's division!

DAISAKU IKEDA,
SGI President,
Together with my wife, Kaneko

Advance Along the Great
Path of Your Noble Mission

JULY 10, 2009: FOR THE MEN'S CONFERENCE
AT THE FLORIDA NATURE AND CULTURE CENTER

TO MY DEAR COMRADES of the SGI-USA men's division! I truly congratulate all of you, representing men throughout America, on having gathered at the FNCC, centering on General Director Danny Nagashima and Men's Leader Tariq Hasan! Please have a most cheerful, exciting and meaningful conference. I am praying that this gathering of hope and victory will ensure the further development of the SGI-USA men's division and reveal immeasurable fortune and virtue within each of you.

Nichiren Daishonin states, "When the skies are clear, the ground is illuminated. Similarly, when one knows the Lotus Sutra, one understands the meaning of all worldly affairs" (WND-1, 376). Once the sun rises and sheds its light, everything is illuminated. Likewise, those who embrace the great Mystic Law also must be versed in worldly affairs. This practice causes the sun of wisdom to rise in our lives, leading us to absolutely win in society and lead victorious lives. As we live our most valuable and precious lives, we simultaneously contribute to our community and society; this is the exact purpose of our practice. Please be convinced that you are the most significant and irreplaceable practitioners, each with a noble individual mission.

Life is a long journey. We will experience rainy days at times and cloudy days at other times. However, the sun is always shining brightly above the clouds. I urge you, the golden pillars of American kosen-rufu, to advance along the great path of your noble missions together with me, chanting Nam-myoho-renge-kyo resonantly, no matter what happens.

I earnestly pray that all of you, the men of the SGI-USA, will live the most wonderful, fulfilled lives, basing yourselves on this practice and showing victorious proof at home and in society. I ask you to forge ahead as great role models in the beautiful unity of "many in body, one in mind," leading the kosen-rufu movement of the world.

Please take good care of yourselves. I am praying for the excellent health and further achievement of each and every one of you. Please give my warmest regards to your comrades in faith and family members when you return home.

Unleash the Great Force of the Buddha

August 2008: For the SGI-USA
Men's Commemorative Meetings

To my respected and cherished members of the men's division, the golden pillars of American kosen-rufu! I greatly appreciate your efforts to hold your conference in commemoration of men's division's month, August.

You are true heroes of kosen-rufu! You strive patiently and bravely day and night for the propagation of Buddhism while overcoming stormy waves in the severe reality of society for the happiness of your family and friends. I sincerely appreciate your continuous efforts. The benefit you will receive through your endeavors will be immeasurable and boundless.

Men are the core of our organization. Men are the most powerful runners of kosen-rufu who will determine its course. Our members feel secure and at ease when they see the dauntless behavior of the men's division members. When your determined voices echo, members gain courage, and can win in all their challenges.

The value of living lies in fulfilling your mission. Nichiren Daishonin states, "Strengthen your faith day by day and month after month" (WND-1, 997). Chant Nam-myoho-renge-kyo resoundingly every day and crown your lives with the greatest happiness and contentment through your shared determination and courageous action.

Through your commitment for kosen-rufu, you can unleash the great force of the Buddha, tap the Buddha wisdom, and see many capable Bodhisattvas of the Earth emerge.

I would like to ask you, the members of the men's division, to overcome every hardship with great composure, taking resolute leadership to guide your respective communities and organizations to clear-cut victory. I hope that you will value the voices of the young women and women to the utmost, giving warm encouragement to the youth division members, your youthful successors. As long as the men's division is in high spirits, the future of American kosen-rufu is sound and solid.

The members of the SGI-USA men's division whom I trust with all my heart! Commence a spectacular, exemplary battle for world-wide kosen-rufu courageously, burning with youthful seeking spirit and filled with abundant life force.

I will earnestly pray for your happiness, good health and the prosperity of your families. Cheers to the SGI-USA men's division members who are the most courageous and intelligent in the entire world!

Continue Your Practice With Strong Faith

JUNE 2008: FOR THE WEST TERRITORY
MEN'S DIVISION KICK-OFF MEETINGS

TO ALL THE MEMBERS OF THE MEN'S division of the West Territory whom I respect, cherish and trust with all my heart! Congratulations on this meeting that signals your new departure!

I have often heard from General Director Nagashima how you have been striving for our shared objective of kosen-rufu. You are true heroes, as you persevere in bravely promoting the propagation of Buddhism for those who are suffering and for the happiness of your beloved families, struggling day and night to cope with the severe reality of the conditions in today's society. The benefit you will gain through your dedicated efforts will shine brilliantly forever.

Our circumstances are constantly changing. I am certain that many of you are facing hardships. When one takes faith in the Lotus Sutra, Nichiren Daishonin teaches that one's misfortune will change into fortune. As long as you continue to chant without doubting the Gohonzon, no matter what may happen to you, and as long as you continue your practice with strong faith for the sake of kosen-rufu, you will be able to tap the great Buddha wisdom and fully utilize every changing phenomenon to win in life and generate hope for your future. This is how you can build indestructible happiness within your lives.

My fellow members of the men's division! Convinced that Buddhism concerns itself with victory or defeat, I hope that you will overcome every adversity brightly, composedly and courageously, taking wise, dauntless and excellent leadership as golden pillars of kosen-rufu while expanding the circles of trust in your communities and society. Please always respect the voices of the women's division members and give warm encouragement to the youth.

Together with me, please create a victorious drama of mentor and disciple, burning with youthful seeking spirit. I am earnestly sending

Nam-myoho-renge-kyo to you with the prayer that each and every one of you, without a single exception, will hoist the flag of victory in society and forge on along the glorious path of total fulfillment as a human being. Please convey my warmest regards to your family members.

Cheers to the pioneers of kosen-rufu who are the most courageous in the world! Again, cheers to all of you!

Men Who Set the Example

August 2006: For the SGI-USA Men's Commemorative Meetings

To my respected and cherished members of the men's division, the golden pillars of American kosen-rufu: My sincere congratulations on the training courses and general meetings being held in various parts of the United States!

Overcoming the harsh waves amid the severe realities of society, you have been struggling day and night with patience and courage for the happiness of your SGI-USA members and for the advancement of kosen-rufu. You are truly great heroes of kosen-rufu. I wholeheartedly admire your painstaking efforts. The benefit you will gain from those endeavors will be boundless and eternal.

Nichiren Daishonin writes, "Strengthen your faith day by day and month after month" (WND-1, 997). Genuine victory will arise from your chanting Nam-myoho-renge-kyo sincerely and seriously and from your brave and dauntless action, conducted on a day-to-day basis. Your earnest prayers and courageous behavior are the key to adorning your lives with authentic happiness and total fulfillment.

Your great life force of Buddhahood will never fail to emerge as long as you have the great objective of kosen-rufu uppermost in your mind. Your Buddha wisdom will definitely arise when you are focused on the great cause of kosen-rufu. Furthermore, innumerable heavenly gods and benevolent deities will without fail function to protect your noble cause.

Buddhism is concerned with winning or losing. I hope that you, the members of the men's division, will creatively surmount all difficulties with composure. In so doing, I hope you will guide your communities and organization toward solid victory for the advancement of kosen-rufu. While cherishing the voices of the young women's division and women's division members to the utmost, please extend warm encouragement to the youth division, the young successors of our movement. As long as the men's division is in high spirits, the future of American kosen-rufu is boundlessly auspicious.

Members of the men's division, whom I trust with all my heart: With a youthful seeking spirit and our lives brimming with vitality, the time has come for us to gallantly commence our splendid struggle for kosen-rufu that is exemplary to the rest of the world.

I am earnestly praying for your happiness, good health and the prosperity of your family. Cheers to the men's division of the SGI-USA!

(August 25, 2006, World Tribune, *p. 1)*

Expand the Circle of Trust and Friendship

August 2000: For the SGI-USA Men's Commemorative Meetings

My sincerest congratulations for your wonderful SGI-USA men's division commemorative meetings! I want to express my heartfelt respect for your daily efforts.

Nichiren Daishonin states, "Be considerate of those who believe in Nichiren and the Lotus Sutra, no matter what they may have done in the past. . . . Always maintain friendly relations with them" (WND-1, 850). In the spirit of this passage, please continue to embrace, love and encourage your fellow members in the world of the SGI, a reflection of society. My hope is that you are always friendly to one another and continue cheerfully building a heart-warming, harmonious human society.

The men's division is pivotal for unity. Only when the center is solid can people harmonize with one another.

I hope that all the members of the SGI-USA men's division are regarded as reliable by their fellow members, listening carefully to women's opinions, embracing everybody and taking full and final responsibility in everything. It is my wish that you will, with strong faith, take courageous leadership in a manner that allows every member to express his or her full potential without reservation. As excellent citizens, please expand the circle of trust and friendship in your respective communities.

I, too, am a member of the men's division, and I am personally determined to fight and forge on with an ever more youthful spirit. Let's fight on bravely together. I seriously pray every day for your good health and long lives and the peace of your families. Please stay in good health forever.

(September 15, 2000, World Tribune, *p. 1)*

Index

A
Abutsu-bo, 18
action(s), 11–12, 16, (20), 48, 52, 70, 74, 77
adversity, 51–52
arrogance, 24, 53–54, 56–58
"attaining Buddhahood as an ordinary person," 50

B
behavior, 10, 12, 51, 53–55, 59, 61, 78–79
behind-the-scenes groups, 7–8, 24
benefit, 23, 31, 35, 74, 77–78
Bodhisattvas of the Earth, 68, 74
Bolívar, Simón, 59–60
Browning, Robert, 30
Buddha, 35
Buddhahood, 14, 24, 77
Buddhism, 10, 35, 68, 70, 76, 78

C
challenging spirit, 22
champion(s), 16–17
change, 63
Common Sense (Paine), 15
complacency, 69
corrupt, 24
courage, 16, 35, 57, 70–71, 77
cowardice, 23, 31
creativity, 13–14

D
Daibyakurenge, 11
dedication, 6
descendants, 34
determination, 18, 35, 57, 69, 72, 74
devilish functions, 50, 58–59
doctors division, 56–57
Du Fu, 18

E
encouragement, 13, 26, 28, 30, 36

F
faith, 8, 28, 30, 49–50, 61, 70–71, 76, 79
family, 10
Federal University of Rondônia, 49
fighting spirit, 61
financial crisis, 29
forbearance, 14
foster, 22–23, 33, 60, 70, 74–76, 78
four sufferings, 10
four virtues, 10
friends, 24
friendship, 79

G
Gandhi, Mahatma, 35, 51
ginkgo (tree), 26–28
Goethe, Johann Wolfgang, 27
goals, 11–12, 63
Gohonzon, 69, 76
good causes, 35